"This is not a pretty part of American history. . . .
But it is important that we try to understand the
villains as well as the heroes in our past, if we
are to continue building a nation where equality
and democracy are preserved."

—JULIAN BOND, CIVIL RIGHTS ACTIVIST
AND PRESIDENT EMERITUS OF THE
SOUTHERN POVERTY LAW CENTER

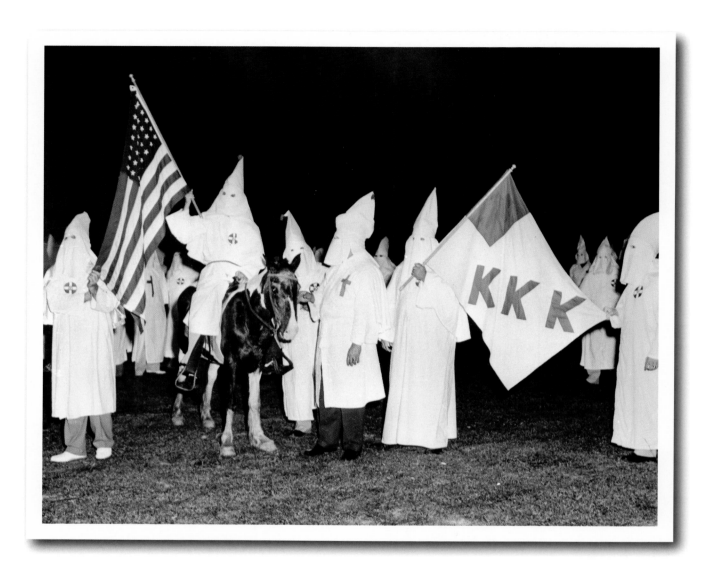

THE KU KLUX KLAN:
A HOODED
BROTHERHOOD

BY ANN HEINRICHS

The Child's World

Published in the United States of America by The Child's World®
PO Box 326
Chanhassen, MN 55317-0326
800-599-READ
www.childsworld.com

The Child's World®: Mary Berendes, Publishing Director
Editorial Directions, Inc.: E. Russell Primm, Emily Dolbear, and Lucia Raatma,
Editors; Linda S. Koutris, Photo Selector; Dawn Friedman, Photo Researcher; Red Line Editorial,
Fact Researcher; Irene Keller, Copy Editor; Tim Griffin/IndexServ, Indexer;
Melissa McDaniel, Proofreader

Cover photograph: An initiation of new Ku Klux Klan members in Jacksonville, Florida/ © Bettmann/Corbis

Interior photographs ©: AP/Wide World Photos: 9, 28; Library of Congress/AP/Wide World Photos: 23;
Jack Smith/AP/Wide World Photos: 32; Mark Foley/AP/Wide World Photos: 33, 34; Alan Steiner,
Coeur d'Alene Press/AP/Wide World Photos: 35; Corbis: 17, 19; Jim McDonald/Corbis: 6; Bettmann/
Corbis: 2, 11, 20, 22, 26, 31; Philip Gould/Corbis: 30; O'Brien Productions/Corbis: 36; Hulton Archive/
Getty Images: 16, 21, 24, 25, 29; North Wind Picture Archives: 10, 12, 13, 14, 15, 18.

Library of Congress Cataloging-in-Publication Data
Heinrichs, Ann.
The Ku Klux Klan : a hooded brotherhood / by Ann Heinrichs.
p. cm. — (Journey to freedom)
Includes index.
Summary: Briefly introduces the origins, history, actions, and impact of the Ku Klux Klan,
a hate group that targets a wide range of ethnic, religious, and cultural groups in the United States.
ISBN 1-56766-646-9 (lib. bdg. : alk. paper)
1. Ku-Klux Klan (1866–1869)—Juvenile literature. 2. Ku Klux Klan (1915–)—Juvenile literature.
3. Racism—United States—History—Juvenile literature. 4. Hate groups—United States—History—Juvenile
literature. 5. United States—Race relations—Juvenile literature. [1. Ku-Klux Klan (1866–1869)
2. Ku Klux Klan (1915–) 3. Racism. 4. Hate groups. 5. Race relations.] I. Title. II. Series.
HS2330.K63 H453 2002
322.4'2'0973—dc21
2001007940

Contents

Ku Klux Klan members strike fear into minority groups in a number of ways. Burning crosses is one practice they use to harass their victims.

A Reign of Terror

A tall wooden cross stands in the clearing. Night is falling as people arrive by car, pickup truck, and motorcycle. At a signal from the leader, they put on white robes, hats, and masks. The leader gives a speech about how minorities are ruining the country. The longer he speaks, the more excited the crowd becomes. Soon they are shouting slogans filled with anger and hate. Their fiery feelings seem to take shape in an eerie ritual as they light torches and march around the cross. Next, they toss their torches to the base of the cross. Then they stand in reverent silence as flames from the burning cross leap to the sky.

This scene is a typical Ku Klux Klan rally. It could be taking place almost anywhere in the United States.

The Ku Klux Klan is one of America's oldest **terrorist** groups. It first appeared after the American Civil War (1861–1865). The war left the South in ruins. Many people had lost homes, farms, friends, and family members. In addition, their former slaves were now free. White people were nervous and fearful of these new citizens in their midst. That fear gave life to the Ku Klux Klan.

The Ku Klux Klan started innocently enough. It began as a sort of silly social club. In less than a year, however, it grew into a lawless terrorist group. Within a few years, interest in the Klan died. However, a new Ku Klux Klan rose up in the twentieth century. This group went far beyond the reach of the original Klan. Its targets were a wide range of ethnic, religious, and cultural groups.

Today, the Ku Klux Klan is just one of many hate groups in the United States. These groups threaten not only their victims, but our nation's most basic principles.

The Birth of the Klan

One evening in December 1865, six young men sat around the fireplace in a law office in Pulaski, Tennessee. All six had served in the Confederate army. Compared to their army days, life was boring now. Jobs were scarce, and there was nothing much to do. The young men decided to form a social club.

Above all, they wanted their club to be secret and mysterious. They invented secret handshakes and passwords. No one was to reveal the secrets or the names of members. In searching for a name, they came up with "Ku Klux." It was based on the Greek word *kyklos,* meaning "circle." One member added the word "Klan" because it sounded good.

At best, the Ku Klux Klan hoped to make mischief and have fun. The young men galloped around Pulaski at night with sheets over their heads. Once they added spooky masks and tall, pointed caps, their uniform was complete. If anyone asked who they were, they said they were the ghosts of dead Confederate soldiers.

The Ku Klux Klan's antics were a great success. That is—they got a lot of attention. Townspeople were startled and scared, and everyone was talking about them. None of the founders expected their club to grow and spread as it did. As one founder wrote, the members thought the Klan would "have its little day and die."

But this was not to be. Soon, young men from surrounding towns wanted to join the Ku Klux Klan. The mystery, secrecy, and shock value were quite exciting. They set up their own local chapters, or "dens," across the Tennessee countryside.

Throughout 1866, the Ku Klux Klan spread quickly to other southern states. Just as quickly, it spun far beyond the control of its founders. The Klansmen enjoyed frightening people. It gave them a sense of power. They decided to use their power to enforce the law as they saw fit.

THE FIRST KLAN COSTUMES WERE NOT ALWAYS WHITE. BUT MEMBERS USUALLY WORE MASKS AND POINTED CAPS.

MEMBERS OF THE KU KLUX KLAN MEETING TOGETHER IN SECRET IN 1871.
THEY WERE PLANNING THE MURDER OF A BLACK MAN IN NORTH CAROLINA.

KU KLUX KLAN VIGILANTES TOOK THE LAW INTO THEIR OWN HANDS. THEY CLAIMED TO BE PROTECTING THEIR COMMUNITIES FROM LAWBREAKERS.

Lawlessness was a problem in the South at this time. Like the economy, law enforcement was in a shambles. Criminals knew they could get away with anything. They roamed the countryside, robbing people and destroying property.

Many Southern communities organized **vigilante** groups for protection. Vigilante groups had been common in frontier days. The new vigilante groups—including the Ku Klux Klan—hunted down lawbreakers and carried out "justice" on their own.

SOMETIMES THE KLAN MEMBERS WOULD FORCE
THEIR WAY INTO THE HOMES OF AFRICAN-AMERICANS.

A GATHERING OF FORMER SLAVES AFTER THE CIVIL WAR. SOME WHITE PEOPLE FELT THREATENED BY THIS NEW GROUP OF AFRICAN-AMERICAN CITIZENS.

To many southerners, the freed slaves were a law-enforcement problem, too. Black people were now free citizens. Many communities suddenly had as many black citizens as white citizens. Some white people saw blacks as a threat to their way of life. Others were afraid blacks would take revenge for their lives in slavery. Naturally, the Ku Klux Klan began to focus their terror on the former slaves.

NIGHT RIDES WERE ONE WAY TO KEEP AFRICAN-AMERICANS AFRAID AND OBEDIENT. THESE NIGHTLY VISITS SOMETIMES ENDED IN VIOLENCE.

"Night rides" were familiar in the plantation culture. They were a way to prevent slave rebellions and escapes. The plantation owner had horsemen ride past the slave quarters at night, making a frightful racket. This was designed to frighten slaves into staying home and being obedient.

The Ku Klux Klan carried on this tradition. At first, they aimed only to frighten blacks. It wasn't long, though, before the night riders moved on to threats and violence. For many white southerners, it was reassuring to have the Klan around for "protection" against their fears.

Reconstruction

As the Ku Klux Klan was rising, the U.S. Congress was gaining more members who were called Radical Republicans. These representatives called for a Reconstruction, or rebuilding, of the South. Some wanted to punish the South for causing the Civil War. Others wanted to reorganize the governments of southern states so that blacks had an equal voice.

In January 1867, Congress passed the first of its Reconstruction Acts. It divided the South into military districts occupied by federal troops. The troops were to register black voters and organize new elections. Each state was to draw up a new state constitution allowing black men to vote. The troops took over state capitols and drove out existing governors. New elections brought in officials who agreed with Reconstruction principles.

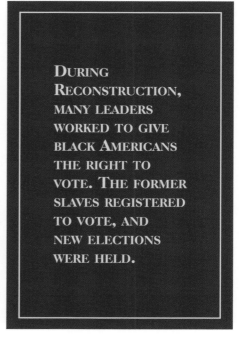

DURING RECONSTRUCTION, MANY LEADERS WORKED TO GIVE BLACK AMERICANS THE RIGHT TO VOTE. THE FORMER SLAVES REGISTERED TO VOTE, AND NEW ELECTIONS WERE HELD.

With Reconstruction, the Ku Klux Klan became more organized and serious. In April 1867, all local Klan groups met in Nashville, Tennessee. The Klan had become famous by now, and members of other vigilante groups joined in, too. Nathan Bedford Forrest was chosen as the Grand Wizard, or leader. Forrest had been a respected cavalry general in the Confederate army.

With Forrest in charge, the Ku Klux Klan agreed on a basic belief in **white supremacy**. It is not known what else the leaders agreed upon. In any case, thousands of white men across the South were Klansmen by this time. And actually, anyone who owned a sheet and a horse could stage a "night ride" in the name of the Klan.

Author Pauli Murray described her grandmother's terror when the Ku Klux Klan came riding by:

"Late at night she would be awakened by the thudding of horses' hooves as night riders, brandishing torches and yelling like banshees, swept into the clearing and rode round and round her cabin, churning the soil outside her door. She never knew when they might set fire to the place, burning her to death inside. . . ."

NATHAN BEDFORD FORREST SERVED AS GRAND WIZARD OF THE KU KLUX KLAN AFTER THE CIVIL WAR.

In this case, the night riders hoped to run the families of black farmers off their land. Other Klansmen aimed to frighten blacks away from voting booths. Klansmen also tried to get rid of black business owners and whites who worked for racial equality. Often the Klan began a project with "warnings." A warning could be a threatening letter. Or a warning could be a wooden cross erected in front of a home and set on fire. (Today, burning a cross to harass someone is against civil rights laws.)

If the warning didn't work, the Klan moved on to violence. They beat, whipped, or tortured their victim. If this failed, they lynched the person. A **lynching** is a murder by a mob of people, and hanging was the most common method. Hanging the body in the center of town served as a message to others. For those who admired the Klan, it was a sign of power and pride.

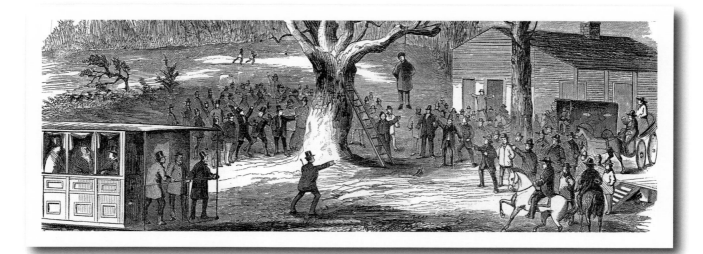

LYNCHING WAS A MOB ACTION THAT RESULTED IN MURDER—USUALLY BY HANGING.

A GROUP OF PEOPLE ORGANIZED FOR A LYNCHING.
SUCH A PUBLIC METHOD OF KILLING MADE POTENTIAL
VICTIMS ALL THE MORE FEARFUL.

Maybe Nathan Bedford Forrest was shocked by the Klan's increasing violence. Or maybe he didn't want to be held responsible for its lawless acts. In any case, he declared the Klan disbanded in 1869. By then, however, the Klan had a life of its own, fueled by hatred and fear.

Reports of the Klan's activities were spreading around the country. President Ulysses S. Grant called for an investigation. In 1871, Congress passed the Ku Klux Klan Act. It was a tough law that put serious crimes under the authority of the federal government. Making night rides and even wearing masks were forbidden. Under this law, hundreds of Klansmen were arrested.

By about 1877, the Ku Klux Klan was seriously weakened. Federal laws had put many of the local leaders and organizations out of commission. But the Klan had accomplished many of its goals by this time. Reconstruction was over, and the old-style state governments were back in place. People could rest assured that blacks would "stay in their place," too.

PRESIDENT ULYSSES S. GRANT WORKED TO BREAK UP THE KU KLUX KLAN. UNDER HIS LEADERSHIP, LAWS WERE PASSED TO ARREST KLANSMEN AND OUTLAW THEIR ACTIVITIES.

WITH A SECRET MEETING IN NOVEMBER 1915, THE KLAN WAS REBORN.
PEOPLE OF MANY BACKGROUNDS AND RACES WERE TARGETED BY THE
NEW GROUP.

The Klan Rises Again

William J. Simmons of Atlanta, Georgia, founded the second Ku Klux Klan. Simmons was a former preacher. On the day before Thanksgiving in 1915, he gathered together a band of fifteen men. They drove up to Georgia's Stone Mountain for their first meeting. There, dressed in white robes and pointed hats, they put up a wooden cross and set it on fire. The Ku Klux Klan was born again.

Feelings around the country were ripe for Simmons's organization. Patriotism was running high during World War I (1914–1918). Many Americans were suspicious of anyone who seemed to be un-American. Such a general description covered a lot of people. Hundreds of thousands of new immigrants had come to the United States in the late 1800s from all over the world.

U.S. TROOPS MARCHING THROUGH LONDON DURING WORLD WAR I. PATRIOTISM FUELED THE EFFORTS OF THE NEW KU KLUX KLAN.

The new Ku Klux Klan targeted not only blacks, but also Jews, Catholics, foreigners, labor-union organizers, and communists. People who were considered immoral were targets, too. That included divorced women and those who campaigned for women's rights. The safest person to be was a white Protestant living a conservative, traditional life.

MANY WOMEN, INCLUDING THOSE WHO WERE DIVORCED AND THOSE WORKING FOR THEIR VOTING RIGHTS, WERE SEEN AS A THREAT BY THE KLAN.

The Klan also drew inspiration from *The Birth of a Nation,* an epic film directed by D. W. Griffith. This 1915 movie is a landmark in filmmaking history. Griffith used it to show off dramatic new camera techniques and special effects. However, the film also showed Klansmen as romantic heroes who saved the South from corrupt Republicans and blacks. *The Birth of a Nation* inspired protests, riots, and lawsuits across the country. Nevertheless, it broke all box-office records of the time. Even today, the Ku Klux Klan uses this film to attract and inspire new members.

The new Klan had a nationwide appeal. Klansmen were elected to local and state government offices and the U.S. Congress. Klan members were especially powerful in Texas, Oklahoma, Indiana, Oregon, and Maine. The organization reached its peak in the mid-1920s, with as many as 4 million members.

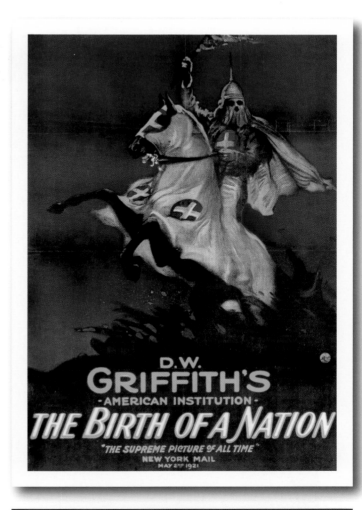

D.W. GRIFFITH'S
- AMERICAN INSTITUTION -
THE BIRTH OF A NATION
"THE SUPREME PICTURE OF ALL TIME"
NEW YORK MAIL
MAY 2ND 1921

THE BIRTH OF A NATION WAS AN IMPORTANT FILM FOR TECHNICAL REASONS. ITS PORTRAYAL OF KU KLUX KLAN MEMBERS AS HEROES ANGERED SOME AND INSPIRED OTHERS.

KU KLUX KLAN MEMBERS ACCEPTING A NEW RECRUIT INTO THEIR GROUP. BY THE MID-1920S, THE KLAN HAD MORE THAN 4 MILLION MEMBERS.

Author Robert Coughlan grew up in Kokomo, Indiana, during that time. "Literally half the town belonged to the Klan when I was a boy," he wrote. "It packed the police and fire departments with its own people, with the result that on parade nights the traffic patrolmen disappeared and traffic control was taken over by sheeted figures."

As in the past, the Klan carried out its "justice" through lynchings. Based on newspaper reports, the Tuskegee Institute of Alabama kept records of lynchings throughout the country. From 1915 to 1935, the institute recorded a total of 726 lynchings. Of those, 654 victims were black and 72 were white. Of course, lynchings that were never reported in newspapers were not counted.

In time, public opinion began to turn against the Klan. People grew tired of seeing the white-robed troublemakers and their burning crosses in their communities. Newspapers also were reporting more and more Klan horrors. Politicians began to realize that the Ku Klux Klan was not such a good ally to have. Klan membership dropped, and those people who remained in the Klan kept a low profile.

KLANSMEN CRAWLING OUT OF A TUNNEL AFTER A SECRET MEETING. MANY MEMBERS HELD POSITIONS IN THEIR COMMUNITIES AND IN GOVERNMENT, SO THEY KEPT THEIR IDENTITIES HIDDEN.

LAWS PASSED IN THE 1950S CALLED FOR THE INTEGRATION OF PUBLIC SCHOOLS. SUCH CHANGES MADE MANY PEOPLE WORRIED AND AFRAID.

The Civil Rights Era

In the 1950s and 1960s, the Ku Klux Klan found a new reason to live. The civil rights movement was a growing force in American life, especially in the South. In 1954, the U.S. Supreme Court ordered that all public schools had to be racially integrated. Again, many white people were tense and fearful about this change.

In the 1960s, white civil rights workers joined southern blacks in their drive for equality. Sometimes they marched down city streets. Sometimes they took freedom rides; that is, blacks and whites rode buses together to protest racial inequality. At the same time, membership in the Ku Klux Klan began to grow again. Klan members went on the attack. They beat the marchers with bats and clubs. They torched freedom riders' buses, burned down the homes of civil rights leaders, and bombed churches.

In Mississippi, the White Knights of the Ku Klux Klan were especially brutal. One night in 1964, they gunned down three civil rights workers in Neshoba County, Mississippi. It was easy because they had the help of local law-enforcement officers. The county sheriff and his deputy helped other Klansmen find and trap the workers.

At first, no murder charges were filed. Then, after three years, the Federal Bureau of Investigation (FBI) tracked down the killers. The 1988 movie *Mississippi Burning* tells the story of the hunt. A jury found only seven of the eighteen accused Klansmen guilty. In 1999, the state of Mississippi began reviewing the case because so much evidence had been overlooked.

THE 16TH STREET BAPTIST CHURCH AFTER IT WAS BOMBED BY THE KLAN IN 1963. FOUR YOUNG BLACK GIRLS DIED IN THE EXPLOSION.

The Ku Klux Klan of the 1960s also used dynamite as a weapon of terror. Klansmen carried out dozens of **arsons** and church bombings throughout the South. In 1963, they dynamited the 16th Street Baptist Church in Birmingham, Alabama. Four young black girls were killed in the explosion. At last, in 2001 and 2002, two former Ku Klux Klan members were convicted of murder in that case.

The FBI began secret operations against the Klan in 1964. Two thousand FBI spies attended Ku Klux Klan meetings and gathered information. In 1965, President Lyndon B. Johnson asked the U.S. Congress to investigate the Ku Klux Klan. Thanks to the FBI and Congress, many Klan leaders were imprisoned. The Klan's power was broken, and members drifted away. Unfortunately, many of the old fears and hatreds stayed alive.

Victories and Defeats

The Ku Klux Klan had another revival in the 1970s. This time, David Duke of Louisiana gave the Klan a new image. He was young, clean-cut, and well-dressed. To promote his views, Duke appeared on television and radio talk shows around the country. He presented the Ku Klux Klan as a nice, respectable organization. Duke appealed to a young, middle-class audience, and the Klan began to grow again. Duke was even elected to the Louisiana state legislature in 1989.

In Alabama, a new Ku Klux Klan group arose around 1980. It was called the Invisible Empire. Its members wielded machine guns and bragged about their military strength. They worked hard to bring teenagers and even younger people into their organization. In summer camps, they trained children in weapons use and racist thinking.

DAVID DUKE, YOUNG AND WELL-DRESSED, REPRESENTED THE NEW KLAN OF THE 1970S AND 1980S. HE WAS EVEN ELECTED TO THE LOUISIANA LEGISLATURE.

The Invisible Empire, a new group in the Ku Klux Klan, was created around 1980. This group encouraged young members and trained them in violence and racism.

Meanwhile, lawyer Morris Dees and other civil rights workers founded the Southern Poverty Law Center (SPLC) in Alabama. The purpose of this organization was to cut down on racial violence through lawsuits and court orders. One of its earliest victories took place in Alabama.

In 1981, a black man in Mobile, Alabama, was on trial for killing a policeman. Because the jury was not able to reach a **verdict**, the man was freed. The local Klan leader held a meeting and declared, "If a black man can get away with killing a white man, we ought to be able to get away with killing a black man."

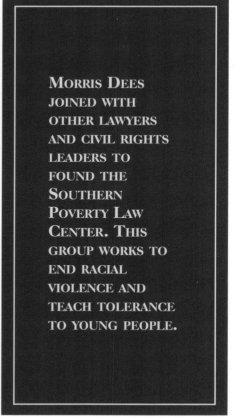

MORRIS DEES JOINED WITH OTHER LAWYERS AND CIVIL RIGHTS LEADERS TO FOUND THE SOUTHERN POVERTY LAW CENTER. THIS GROUP WORKS TO END RACIAL VIOLENCE AND TEACH TOLERANCE TO YOUNG PEOPLE.

Two young Klansmen, aged seventeen and twenty-six, decided to put this into action. That night, they got a gun and a rope and went out hunting for a black man. They found nineteen-year-old Michael Donald walking home from his cousin's house. They bashed him to death with a tree limb, slit his throat, and hung his body from a tree.

THE FUNERAL OF MICHAEL DONALD. HUNDREDS GATHERED TO PAY RESPECTS TO THIS INNOCENT YOUNG BLACK MAN WHO WAS MURDERED BY THE KU KLUX KLAN IN 1981.

The local police easily got rid of the case. They claimed Michael had been killed in a bad drug deal. However, Beulah Mae Donald, Michael's mother, would not let the case die. Through her efforts, the FBI went to Alabama and did its own investigation. The two young men were caught and tried. One received life imprisonment, and the other got the death penalty. It was the first time since 1913 that a white person in Alabama was executed for killing a black person.

Mrs. Donald did not stop at that. She wanted the Ku Klux Klan to stand trial, too. With the help of the SPLC, she sued the Alabama Klan for civil rights violations. The all-white jury found the Klan guilty and fined it $7 million. This was just one of many victories the SPLC would score against the Klan.

BEULAH MAE DONALD AT THE FUNERAL OF HER SON. WITH THE HELP OF THE SOUTHERN POVERTY LAW CENTER, MRS. DONALD SAW HER SON'S KILLERS BROUGHT TO JUSTICE.

A Larger Picture of Hate

In the mid-1980s, the Ku Klux Klan itself began to become a minority. One after another, new hate groups sprang up around the country. Their aims ranged from white power to overthrowing the U.S. government. Their methods ranged from hate-based radio talk shows to bombings and murders. Victims included not only blacks but also Jews, Muslims, Asians, Hispanics, Native Americans, and homosexuals.

People who thrived on hate now had plenty of choices if they wanted company. **Neo-Nazi** groups revived the anti-Jewish beliefs of Adolf Hitler, Germany's leader in the 1930s and 1940s. The Skinheads were a similar racist group. The White Aryan Resistance (WAR) and the Aryan Nations were leaders in white supremacy. Many Ku Klux Klan members joined other groups in addition to the Klan.

THE ARYAN NATIONS BELIEVE IN WHITE SUPREMACY AND ARE AMONG A NUMBER OF HATE GROUPS THAT HAVE FORMED IN THE PAST SEVERAL DECADES.

By the early twenty-first century, hate groups were active all over the country. In 2000, the Southern Poverty Law Center listed more than 600 active hate groups. Of these, 110 were Ku Klux Klan chapters in twenty-four states. They ranged from California in the west to Delaware in the east, from Wisconsin in the north to Florida in the south.

It's hard to keep track of all the different Ku Klux Klan groups today. As members disagree on goals and methods, they split into rival groups. Unfortunately, the Internet has become a useful tool for finding new members.

Klan leaders do their best to make their message attractive. They say they are only trying to keep the country safe. But the country will never be safe without the rights guaranteed in the U.S. Constitution. These include every American's right to "life, liberty, and the pursuit of happiness."

IN SPITE OF THE KU KLUX KLAN AND OTHER HATE GROUPS, MANY PEOPLE IN THE UNITED STATES WORK TO ENSURE EQUAL RIGHTS FOR ALL OF ITS CITIZENS.

Timeline

1865	Former Confederate soldiers start the Ku Klux Klan as a social club.
1867	Congress passes the first Reconstruction Act; the Ku Klux Klan is formally organized, with Nathan Bedford Forrest in command.
1869	Forrest orders the Ku Klux Klan to be disbanded.
1871	The U.S. Congress passes the Ku Klux Klan Act to stop Klan terror.
1892	The United States records the highest number of lynchings in one year. The 230 victims include 161 blacks and 69 whites.
1915	William J. Simmons organizes a new Ku Klux Klan in Georgia; the film *Birth of a Nation* is released.
1920s	Ku Klux Klan members hold high offices in several states. Membership in the Klan reaches its highest point, with as many as 4 million members.
1963	Klan members bomb a Baptist church in Birmingham, Alabama, killing four girls.
1964	Klan members kill three civil rights workers in Mississippi.

1965	President Lyndon B. Johnson begins a congressional investigation of the Ku Klux Klan
1971	Lawyer Morris Dees founds the Southern Poverty Law Center. Its purpose is to gather information on racial violence and to combat it through education and lawsuits.
1980s	The Skinhead racist movement begins organizing members in the United States.
1984	The White Aryan Resistance group begins broadcasting a racist radio talk show.
1987	An Alabama jury brings a $7 million judgment against the United Klans of America for the 1981 murder of a black youth in Mobile.
1999	The state of Mississippi reopens the case against the 1964 Klan murders of three civil rights workers.
2001	A former Ku Klux Klan member is convicted of murder in the 1963 Birmingham church-bombing case.
2002	Another former Klansman is convicted of murder in the Birmingham church-bombing case.

Glossary

arsons (AHR-suhns)
Arsons are acts of burning property with criminal intent. The Ku Klux Klan committed arson throughout the South.

lynching (LINCH-ing)
Lynching is a mob action of killing someone, usually by hanging. The Ku Klux Klan often lynched African-Americans and hanged them in public areas.

neo-Nazi (NEE-oh NAHT-see)
A neo-Nazi is someone who adopts the beliefs of Adolf Hitler's Nazi Party of 1930s and 1940s Germany. Neo-Nazis are another kind of hate group.

terrorist (TER-ur-ist)
A terrorist is someone who tries to control others through fear and acts of violence. The Ku Klux Klan is one type of terrorist group.

verdict (VUR-dikt)
A verdict is the decision of a jury about whether someone is guilty or innocent of a crime. Some juries are unable to reach verdicts, so new trials are ordered or people on trial are set free.

vigilante (vij-uh-LAHN-tee)
A vigilante is a member of a volunteer group formed to keep law and order and to punish real or imagined crimes. After the Civil War, the Ku Klux Klan was one kind of vigilante group.

white supremacy (WHYT suh-PREM-uh-see)
White supremacy is the idea that white people are superior to people of other races. Members of the Ku Klux Klan believe in white supremacy.

Index

FOR FURTHER READING

Books

Anderson, Ken, and Melissa Roberts. *You Can't Do That, Dan Moody!* Austin, Tex.: Eakin, 1998.

Coleman, Evelyn. *Circle of Fire.* Middleton, Wis.: Pleasant Company, 2001.

Cook, Fred J. *The Ku Klux Klan: America's Recurring Nightmare.* New York: Julian Messner, 1989.

Hesse, Karen. *Witness.* New York: Scholastic, 2001.

Web Sites

Visit our homepage for lots of links about the Ku Klux Klan:
http://www.childsworld.com/links.html

Note to Parents, Teachers, and Librarians:
We routinely verify our Web links to make sure they're safe,
active sites—so encourage your readers to check them out!

ABOUT THE AUTHOR

Ann Heinrichs grew up in Fort Smith, Arkansas, and lives in Chicago. She is the author of more than fifty books for children and young adults on Asian, African, and U.S. history and culture. After many years as a children's book editor, she enjoyed a successful career as an advertising copywriter. She has also written numerous newspaper, magazine, and encyclopedia articles.

Ms. Heinrichs holds bachelor's and master's degrees in piano performance. She has traveled widely in the United States, Africa, Asia, and the Middle East. A practitioner of t'ai chi empty-hand and sword forms, she has won a number of awards in martial arts competitions.